Book Synop

C000125530

"Let There Be Sight" is a supern........... g into the realms of dreams and visions, Godly and demonic visitations. Increase your revelation regarding the purpose of prophetic dreams, visions, and mental pictures, and how to interpret, govern, and utilize them effectively in ministry. Gain greater insight on communing with God at night, warring and interceding in dreams, visions and heavenly realms, and how to be proactive in asserting authority over the devil when he attacks you in your dreams, visions, and heavenly realms.

TaquettaBaker@Kingdomshifters.com

(Website) Kingdomshifters.com

Connect with Taquetta via Facebook or YouTube

Copyright 2014 – Kingdom Shifters Ministries

Taquetta's Bio

Taquetta Baker is the founder of Kingdom Shifters Ministries (KSM). She has authored fourteen books and two decree CD's. Taquetta has a Master's Degree in Community Counseling with an emphasis on Marriage, Children and Family Counseling, a Bachelor's Degree in Psychology and Associates Degree in Business Administration. In addition, Taquetta has a Therapon Belief Therapist Certification from Therapon Institute and has 22 years of professional and Christian Counseling experience.

Taquetta is also gifted at empowering and assisting people with launching ministries, businesses and books and provides mentoring, counseling and vision casting through Kingdom Shifters Kingdom Wellness Program. Taquetta serves on the Board of Directors for New Day Community Ministries, Inc. of Muncie, IN. In October 2008, Taquetta graduated from the Eagles Dance Institute under Dr. Pamela Hardy and received her license in liturgical dance. Before launching into her own ministry, Taquetta served at her previous church for 12 years. She was a prophet, pioneer and leader of Shekinah Expressions Dance Ministry, teacher, member of the presbytery board, and overseer of the Altar Workers Ministry. Taquetta receives mentoring and ministry covering from Bishop Jackie Green, Founder of JGM-National PrayerLife Institute (Phoenix, AZ), and was ordained as an Apostle on June 7, 2014.

Taquetta flows through the wells of warfare and worship and mantles an apostolic mandate of judging and establishing God's kingdom in people, ministries, communities, and regions. Taquetta travels in foreign missions and throughout the United States. She has mentored and established dance, altar workers, deliverance, and prophetic ministries. Taquetta ministers in the areas of fine arts, all manners of prayer, fivefold ministry, deliverance, healing, miracles, atmospheric worship, and empowers and train people in their destiny and life's vision.

Connect with Taquetta and KSM at <u>kingdomshifters.com</u> or via Facebook. For more information regarding Bishop Jackie Green at <u>Jgmenternational.org</u>.

TABLE OF CONTENTS

Foreword

"Let There Be Sight" was very enlightening. There were many contents to the revelation of the book that highlighted areas in my own life and helped me acquire breakthrough in the areas of dreams and visions and dealing with dream attacks from the enemy. For instance, Taquetta wrote about shapeshifters and how they take in the form of someone you may know to gain your trust and cause you to be vulnerable in your dreams and visions. As a dreamer, this has happened to me many times in the past and I was succumbing to attacks. However, two nights after reading this book I had a dream, could discern what was occurring. I called out the demonic spirit, and it left my presence.

It is just like John 8:32 says, "We shall know the truth and the truth shall set us free." Once I received revelation through "Let There Be Sight" regarding how dreams and visions operate, how God speaks to me in them, how the enemy infiltrates them and what I was battling, I became keener in being able to govern my dream realms and the demonic spirits that would attack this area of my life lost its power over me.

Now I realize how the enemy uses deception and fear to oppress people, not just in dreams and visions, but in life in general. Once we can see something for what it truly is we can handle it accordingly.

There was additional revelation mentioned in this book that I could relate to. In the past, I have had many dreams, but there have been a few that I always wondered if I was at that place in the natural realm because my senses were more heightened and my experience felt more like real life than a dream. There was one experience had where I walked out of my body and Jesus escorted me around and showed me many things about demons live at people's houses. "Let There Be Sight" gave me clarity about what I was experiencing and provided me greater

revelation on how to discern when I am having a dream and a vision, and when I have been translated to an actual location by the Holy Spirit for the purposes of ministry, warfare, intercession, etc. Overall "Let There Be Sight" was very informative and empowering. I appreciate the opportunity to gleam from the revelation of this book.
Rebecca Lynn Lomax of Muncie, IN, Dreamer & Mentee of Taquetta Baker

Dreams & Visions

Dictionary.com defines "*dream*" as, "*a succession of images, thoughts, or emotions passing through the mind during sleep, an involuntary vision occurring to a person when awake.*"

Dreams tell a story as a sequence of events tend to occur during a dream.

Dictionary.com defines "vision" as, "*an experience in which a personage, thing, or event appears vividly or credibly to the mind, although not actually present, often under the influence of a divine or other agency.*"

A vision is when the eyes open in our imagination and we are watching a movie. Visions can happen at any time as they can occur when a person is sleep, semi-sleep, soaking in the presence of the Lord, resting, prayer, washing dishes or while a person is wide awake and going about the day. We can also have visions within our dreams as sometimes we maybe dreaming and then a vision will manifest inside the dream.

Sometimes a person will receive mental pictures or quick flashes of people, situations, images, etc. When this happens, ask God what He is wanting you to do with what He is showing you.

Dreams, visions and mental pictures can be of God, demonic, or soulish. Some dreams, vision and mental pictures we label as demonic, could be God revealing things about the enemy, principalities and high places in the region, the end times, or could be a word of correction or warning. If you are unsure of which category the dream belongs, ask God if the dream is of Him or not. He will let you know and will lead you in what to do with the dream or vision.

God speak through dreams and visions to:

- Hide His word in our heart
- Reveal our callings and giftings (Genesis 37:5-7)
  Share revelation when we are rested that we are too busy to hear and retain during the day (Job 33:15-26)
- Provoke our Spirit to seek Him for deeper things regarding His word and presence, as dreams require us to dig deep into the mysteries of God
- Release and/or confirm prophecy (Daniel 7, Judges 7:13-14, Genesis 40:5)
- Reveal personal, generational, and regional strongholds
- Reveal future and end time revelation and happenings
- Expose the enemy's camp to us (Matthew 2:19-21)
- Reveal sin issues or warn of potential to sin (Genesis 20:3-7)
- Reveal soul wound issues to us
- Reveal truth (Matthew 27:19)
- Heal, deliver (Judges 7:13-15), warn (Genesis 20:3), empower, commune (1Kings 3:5), reconcile, restore, mend hearts and even relationships, instill reverenced fear (Job 7:14)
- Fulfill the prophecy of Joel regarding His outpouring of dreams and visions (Joel 2:28, Acts 2:17)

Daniel 1:17 - As for these four children, God gave them knowledge and skill in all learning and wisdom: and Daniel had understanding in all visions and dreams.

Just as Daniel, we can have access in understanding all our visions and dreams. It is important not to get frustrated when we do not receive an initial interpretation or revelation of a dream or vision. Frustration blocks us from being able to hear and discern God.

- Some dreams maybe for a specific time and God is just hiding the dream in your heart for a later day.
- Sometimes we are not ready for the interpretation.
- Sometimes we may need to fast and spend time in pray for an interpretation.
- Sometimes our imagination is clogged with mixture and worldly contamination which hinders our interpretation.
- Sometimes we could have been having an actual encounter with God or we are in the spirit realm having an actual experience and no interpretation is needed.
- Sometimes we do not want to acknowledge truth so we seek interpretation when we already know what God is saying.
- Sometimes we fear the interpretation so we are resistant to hearing and being accountable to what will be required of us.
- Sometimes we second guess our interpretation because of our own inadequacy.

As someone who has constant dreams and visions, I assure you that you can read countless books on the subject and should do just that, however, the best teacher for interpreting your dreams and visions and utilizing them in life, and ministry is the Holy Spirit. I state this because there is no true pattern for interpreting dreams. The Holy Spirit may lead you to interpret one way for one dream and then entirely different way for another. The significance to interpreting dreams and visions is being sensitive to the Holy Spirit, while being able to identify the keys in the dreams and visions; and unlocking the mysteries to what the Lord is speaking.

> *Acts 2:17-18 - And it shall come to pass in the last days, God declares, that I will pour out of My Spirit upon all mankind, and your sons and your daughters shall prophesy [telling forth the divine counsels] and your young men shall see visions (divinely granted appearances), and your old men shall dream [divinely suggested] dreams. Yes, and on My menservants also and on My maidservants in those days I will pour out of My Spirit, and they shall prophesy [telling forth the divine counsels and predicting future events pertaining especially to God's kingdom].*

Out is "*cheo*" in the Greek and means:
1. (to pour); to pour forth; figuratively, to bestow
2. gush (pour) out, run greedily (out), shed (abroad, forth), spill
3. shed, shed forth, spill, run out, run greedily, shed abroad
4. metaphor: to bestow or distribute largely

This passage let us know that God expects us to dream and have visions. God says He is pouring out His Spirit. His outpouring suggests that dreams and visions should be endlessly available to us. They should be constant and greedily run in an outpouring into our lives. With them comes prophesy and destiny downloads (dream dreams) that advance the kingdom. We should be dreaming and experiencing visions and we should be receiving answers, revelation, and direction from our dreams and visions. It is important to understand that dreams are real realms. Science contends that we encounter five stages of rest before we enter deep sleep. Though science is unsure of the reason for the stages, they contend that throughout the night we can go in and out of these stages. As we enter a place of rest, our physical body goes to sleep and enters a stage of paralysis. Our brain is still active and is sending signals to our body to ensure we retain the necessary functions to maintain life as we sleep. Stage five is where we encounter REM (rapid eye movement) sleep aka as deep sleep. Though we can have visions and dreams in other stages, the REM stage is where most dreams occur and is where our heart rate increases, as it is pumping blood to our brain and other body parts to maintain life.

Science does not speak of this, we know however, from the bible stating that God who is all Spirit (Psalms 121:3-4), never sleeps or slumbers, so our Spirit never sleeps. And we see from science that our heart is active as well. Our soul is a part of our heart and Spirit so though it can be at peace or rest, it does not sleep either. I would contend that because our heart, soul, and spirit are awake, this is the reason many dreams feel so real - like real encounters. They feel real because they are. Our heart, soul and Spirit are actively engaged in our night season though our body maybe sleep and/or at rest.

- What we expose our heart, soul and spirit to when we are awake, can help determine the realms we enter when we are asleep.
- Also, what we meditate upon before and as we press into sleep can be a factor of the realms we experience.

- Soulish and life/heart issue can also determine the realms we are exposed to when we sleep.
- Because our defenses are down, demons, witches, astral projectors tend to attack when we are sleeping.
- And of course, God can always open sleep realms to us.

Proverbs 4:20-23 - My son, attend to my words; incline thine ear unto my sayings. Let them not depart from thine eyes; keep them in the midst of thine heart. For they are life unto those that find them, and health to all their flesh. Keep thy heart with all diligence; for out of it are the issues of life.

Matthew 12:35 - A good man out of the good treasure of the heart bringeth forth good things: and an evil man out of the evil treasure bringeth forth evil things.

During REM sleep or deep sleep, we are in our most vulnerable realm. I say this because, our body has gone through the process of being at to total rest, and our brain has entered a state where mainly the eyes are active. The eyes are where our imagination is housed. The bible tells us to cast down vain imagination and everything that exalts itself about Him.

2Corinthians 10:4-6 - (For the weapons of our warfare are not carnal, but mighty through God to the pulling down of strong holds); Casting down imaginations, and every high thing that exalteth itself against the knowledge of God, and bringing into captivity every thought to the obedience of Christ.

We assume we are not to have an imagination or we cannot use our imagination. This is error. Imagination is the realm where God speaks to us through dreams, visions, and pictures. It is also the place where we mediate on the image and things of a God.

> **Psalms 1:2** - *But his delight [is] in the law of the LORD; and in his law doth he meditate day and night.*

> **Philippians 4:8** - *Finally, brethren, whatsoever things are true, whatsoever things [are] honest, whatsoever things [are] just, whatsoever things [are] pure, whatsoever things [are] lovely, whatsoever things [are] of good report; if [there be] any virtue, and if [there be] any praise, think on these things.*

> **Psalms 1:1-2** - *Blessed [is] the man that walketh not in the counsel of the ungodly, nor standeth in the way of sinners, nor sitteth in the seat of the scornful. But his delight [is] in the law of the LORD; and in his law doth he meditate day and night.*

The eyes are where our imagination is stored and is where our dreams, visions, and mental pictures occur. As we meditate, our imagination begins to fill up with God images – His character and His nature – and then God begins to use our imagination to download His plan to us through visions and dreams. When our imagination is full of vain glory, worldliness, wickedness, and when we have not effectively meditated and focused on God, He cannot give us His thoughts, pictures, dreams, visions. Our imagination will be consumed with things that are not of Him, and that exalt against the knowledge of who He is in our lives.

> **Ephesians 1:18** - *The eyes of your understanding being enlightened; that ye may know what is the hope of his calling, and what the riches of the glory of his inheritance in the saints.*

Eyes is *"ophthalmos"* in the Greek and means, *"vision, the eyes of the mind, the faculty of knowing."*

<u>Enlightened</u> is *"photizo"* in the Greek and means:
1. to give light, to shine
2. to enlighten, light up, illumine
3. to bring to light, render evident
4. to cause something to exist and thus come to light and become clear to all
5. to enlighten, spiritually, imbue with saving knowledge
6. to instruct, to inform, teach, to give understanding to

Our eyes are where we can discern, know, and see, the path of God. As we are consistently enlightened by mediating (imaging) on the things of God, we are being consumed and activated in His riches and calling for our lives. This is essential to a life of a prayer warrior. Because it will enable the prayer warrior to discern which dreams and visions are from God and which are not. It will also assist the prayer warrior with being able to discern the keys in a dream/vision that are necessary for interpreting and effectively applying what is being revealed to life situations.

When interpreting dreams, visions, mental pictures pay attention to the follow:

- Journal all your dreams/visions, even the demonic and soulish ones. There could be clues in them to thwart the dreams/visions from occurring again
- Though not always the case, a dream can be two or three dimensional. Be open to exploring the dream from these three areas:
  o How it relates to the person having the dream

- How it relates to the people and situations in the dream
- How it relates to the body of Christ and world at large
- Colors (study biblical colors and learn what they mean
- What is occurring in the dream and vision (journal even the little things that you would normally think do not matter – they may hold the greatest keys)
- Who is in the dream/vision (dogs, momma, friend, strangers)
- What were the names (what is the definition of their names –use online search engines to acquire the definition of their name)
- What was in the dream/vision (cars, houses, pictures)
- What was the time of day in the dream/vision and when the dream/vision occurred (morning, noon, night)
- Season the dream/vision took place (winter, spring, summer, fall)
- Where did the dream take place (Texas, in a church, at a park)
- Mood of the dream (gloomy, happy, sunny)
- Mood and characteristics of the person dreaming and those in the dream (happy, sad, depressed, confused, suspicious, controlling, angry)
- Does the dream/vision confirm, reveal, warn, expose, encourage, discourage, set free, bind up, etc.
- What are your initial thoughts when first awaking from the dream, as you journal the dream, and after further exploring the dream
- What scriptures come to mind as you consider the dream/vision
- What experiences, people, situations, places, etc., come to mind as you explore the dream/vision

- Use wisdom on who to acquire interpretation or further exploration of the dream/vision from. It is okay to seek assistance interpreting a dream/vision but make sure it is someone you trust and that is mature in their walk. It can also be someone who has the gift of interpretation
- Only share the dream/vision as the Spirit leads. Sometimes, it is not necessary to share a dream/vision with a person or congregation. Simply share the message or strategy given in a dream/vision. Everyone will not be able to handle what occurred in the dream/vision and it could be a factor with them receiving what God is striving to convey. Seek God regarding what He reveals to you in a dream/vision and follow through with what He says
- When God shows you dreams/visions about your calling and future, be cautious who you share them with. You expect everyone to be happy for you but this is not reality. Joseph's brother threw him in a pit and then sold him into slavery when he shared his dreams with them. If you are just burning to tell someone talk to Jesus about it; though He already knows, He will be happy for you and even empower you in what He has revealed to you (laughing but very serious)
  - If you are unsure about something regarding a dream/vision or forget a part, do not make assumptions or add to the dream/vision. Ask God to reveal the information to you and be okay if He desires not to. Sometimes this information is hidden in your heart for a later season and so God only allows you to remember what is necessary for the present season.
  - Revisit your dreams/visits as some dreams and visions can mean one thing in one season and have a whole other meaning in another season of your

life, the people life that is in the dream/vision or for the body of Christ and world as a whole

Kingdom Keys Visions
(BY: Renita Keys)

This chapter was written by "Renita Keys." Renita is one of Taquetta's Spiritual Daughters. Renita has an exceptional seer gift and has great insight regarding how we are to effectively use our visions and dreams to glorify God and conquer the wiles of the enemy.

Visions are similar to dreams; the only difference is we receive them during the awake period of our day. Visions come in different ways and in encompasses different experiences. The key to unlocking visions is very simple, yet many people find it very hard, because of their encounters with religion and tradition. The key is not limiting God and allowing the Holy Spirit to lead you in understanding and utilizing your visions. When we do this, the Holy Spirit can unlock keys within our heart, mind and spirit that possess the will of Christ in relations to those visions and dreams.

One evening I was seeking the Lord and I asked Him for more clarity on how we can have visions. The Lord began to tell me that when we have visions we are seeing things through His eyes and not our own. So, when we have a vision the Holy Spirit is allowing us to look through the eyes of God. We can search out what the Lord is trying to bring to our attention and establish it in our natural lives. God is omnipresent, which means God is everywhere at the same time. This is how the Lord can speak to us personally and as a body through our eyes, yet each of us experience Him and reveal different fashions of Him. Visions are prophetic messages through the form of an image and holds very important keys and strategies. Therefore, it is very important to write down what we see or even voice record your visions. When we write down or record what we see in the spirit, we are establishing it in the earth realm. Do not make it a habit of waiting until later to write or record your visions because you may forget a very vital key.

> **Habakkuk 2:2** - *And the Lord answered me: "Write the vision; make it plain on tablets, so he may run who reads it.*

Sight is one of the five senses that we have in the natural and we have the same five senses in the spirit. Many are blind in the spirit because they genuinely do not have the eyes of their heart open to receive. This is the very reason why Apostle Paul had prayed for the heart to be enlightened. When the eyes of the heart are enlightened we can see things that are going on in and around us. God wants us to enter the heavens and receive everything we have inherited. It is very important to have faith and have an expectancy in our heart that the Lord will fulfill and deliver.

> **Ephesians 1:18-19** - *I pray that the eyes of your heart may be enlightened in order that you may know the hope to which he has called you, the riches of his glorious inheritance in his holy people, and his incomparably great power for us who believe.*

The more we exercise our senses in the spirit realm the stronger they become windows to our heart, mind and soul.

Visions are not limited to certain people. God wants all of His children to see their inheritance. Some may have the gift of discerning spirits and are able to see into the spirit easier than others, but that does not mean that we must have the gift to have visions. Through the Holy Spirit everyone can experience visions.

Ephesians 3:20 - Now to Him who is able to do exceedingly abundantly above all that we ask or think, according to the power that works in us.

The Holy Spirit lives in us and is the key of our salvation. God is not biased that He would only allow certain children to prophesy, see in the spirit, speak in tongues, hear His voice or receive revelation. He can do exceed abundantly above anything we could ask or think. We must ask the Lord for our eyes to be enlightened and the Holy Spirit will do a work in us to honor the request. Elisha prayed that the eyes of his servant's heart would be enlightened so he could see into the Spirit realm, and God honored Elisha's request.

> *2Kings 6:17 English Standard Version - Then Elisha prayed and said, "O Lord, please open his eyes that he may see." So the Lord opened the eyes of the young man, and he saw, and behold, the mountain was full of horses and chariots of fire all around Elisha.*

> *Matthew 7:7-8 - At times we may make things harder than they really are when we only have to simply ask the Lord. Jesus tells us this from His very mouth in/*

> *English Standard Version - Ask, and it will be given to you; seek, and you will find; knock, and it will be opened to you. For everyone who asks receives, and the one who seeks finds, and to the one who knocks it will be opened.*

If we ask with a pure heart, God will give it to us. You can ask for the eyes of your heart to be opened and He will open your eyes. Once He opens your eyes, diligently seek the Lord so He can show you more than your mind could fathom or make up on its own.

Many people ask that the Lord would allow them to see, but never take a leap of faith and seek to be in a place of being shown anything. Therefore, we should knock on the door of expectation, and expect the door to be opened for greater visitation and demonstration.

Patience To See

Patience is a very valuable key when unlocking your spiritual eyes. You must be in a place of having faith, but also not rushing the Holy Spirit. The Holy Spirit is always doing a work in us. When we ask the Holy Spirit to shine the light of God through our eyes things SHIFT, and the eyes may enter a processing of cleansing and deliverance so they can be healed to see and handle what will be seen.

Many want to see an abundant of visions consistently but we must be trust that the Lord knows how much we are to see and when we are to experience visions. The Lord has allowed me to see ever since I was a child, but I never understood what it was since I did not grow up being taught about the supernatural or gifts. When the Lord opened the eyes of my heart it was as if someone opened a flood gate of visions to me. I was seeing and dreaming continually, and it was very exciting. A month or two later I SHIFTED into a new season and my visions were shut off. I thought I did something wrong against God and I didn't know what was going on. The Lord told me that I SHIFTED into a season of healing. He stopped the flow of visions and dreams so I could solely focus on my healing process that was taking place in my heart. After my healing process, the floodgate of visions has returned and has been constant.

When our eyes are healed and opened, the Lord will also allow us to see the fullness of our gift and where we can grow spiritually to mature in our walk with Him. For this reason, patience with letting God lead and reveal His will for visions is VERY important.

> *Romans 12:12 – English Standard Version* - *Rejoice in hope, be patient in tribulation, be constant in prayer.*

This scripture is telling us to rejoice in the goodness of God because He is everything we could ever ask for. Be patient while we are going through a process in our lives, while consistently praying for the word and promises of God to come to pass. For as we prayer we are birthing things in the Spirit realm knowing or unknowingly and as we rest in patience, God SHIFTS us into what we birthed forth in prayer. Visions are your portion says the Lord.

How To Increase In Experiencing Visions

The Lord will increase visions when we are not fearful. Some may be fearful of the unknown and afraid of what God might show them. They have the mentality that all they will see is evil spirits and things of the demonic realm. That is exactly what the enemy wants you to think. Yes, the Lord will allow you to see these things, but He will only show you what your Spirit is able to handle. The reason we can see angels and demons is because we are discerning spirits. God allow us to see demonic spirits for a reason. When we see them, we can bind, rebuke and wreak havoc upon the enemy's camp.

> *Luke 10:17-19 – New Living Translation* - *When the seventy-two disciples returned, they joyfully reported to him, "Lord, even the demons obey us when we use your name!" "Yes," he told them, "I saw Satan fall from heaven like lightning! Look, I have given you authority over all the power of the enemy, and you can walk among snakes and scorpions and crush them. Nothing will injure you.*

Would not you try to scare someone that has the very blueprint to your secret plans? When my eyes were first opened this happened to me. Even though I have seen things as a child, once I truly gave my life to the Lord, I now had a revelation of everything I was seeing and the purpose to which I was seeing. I was very you in my walk with God and I did not want to see demons and evil spirits. I became fearful of what I might see. I remember the Lord's voice so clear. He told me not to be fear, because I have power and dominion over the demonic realm. After I received that word, demons that I would see on the college campus and in the dorms, started to run away from me in terror. For those who may be wounded or fearful you must walk in the authority God has bestowed onto you, and know that you were given dominion over everywhere your feet tread upon even as you tread as a seer.

Another way to increase your vision is simply spending intimate time with God. When we set aside a time to meet with the Lord, He is eagerly awaiting to commune and enlighten us. God will see the flame of yearning and desire in our heart, and will exceed any expectation with visions and dreams. When you meet in the secret place, you can build relationship with God, and a yearning to delight in what pleases or concerns Him. This is a time of joy, peace, love and just delighting in the presence of the Lord, and allow Him to fill your eyes, ears, heart, and soul with him. As you are delighting in Him your love is being poured out unto Him and His love is being bestowed upon you. He loves when we pour out our love on Him and through our enlightened blissful eyes, we are able to see and discern the promises of His heart.

> *Psalms 37:4 – The Amplified Version* - *Delight yourself also in the Lord, and He will give you the desires and secret petitions of your heart.*

In this time of intimacy, we can focus solely on what the Holy Spirit shows us through words and images.

> *Luke 12:34 – New King James Version - For where your treasure is, there your heart will be also.*

How Visions Manifests

There are different ways we can have visions.   Many have visions when their eyes are closed and there are some that receive more visions with their eyes wide open. When your eyes are wide open and you are seeing in the spirit these are called open visions. When the Lord shows you an image it is very important to for you to seek deeper revelation by searching it out.

- What did He show you?
- What was going on in the vision?
- Were there any significant colors?
- Do you hear a scripture that relates to what you're seeing?

The more you allow the Holy Spirit to take over your imagination, the broader your spiritual sight will become. There are things that you need to be aware of when it comes to spiritual sight. The first thing being distractions. Distractions will come to take distract and steal from what God is trying to show you. Distractions come in the form of thoughts and the things around you. As you are SHIFTING into focusing on the Holy Spirit, you might notice that you start to think of the things you need to do or get done, things that have already happened that day, or you might even have random thoughts. Therefore, we must cast our crowns at the feet of Jesus and these are the things that try to exalt itself above God.

You must be on guard as a warrior and ready to move on God's command. You must be keen and sensitive to the spirit so you can discern what is of God and what is just the enemy trying to deceive. You must wear the helmet of salvation daily, as the enemy would love to taint your thoughts and visions so he can twist or manipulate what God is truly doing for you. The more time you are spending intimate time with God, the greater your discernment will become and you are able to detect distractions when they manifest. The word talks about our discernment being exercised in *Hebrews 5:14*.

> *Hebrews 5:14 – New King James Version* - *But solid food belongs to those who are of full age, that is, those who by reason of use have their senses exercised to discern both good and evil.*

Guarding Your Eyes
Our senses are just like muscles, the more you exercise them the stronger and more defined they are. Being mature in your spiritual senses will allow you to push deeper into the realm of the spirit than you have ever gone before. After all, there is always something new to learn about God.
Being keen will allow you to dismantle the things of the enemy that may try to combat against you. This includes portals, gates and doors. The enemy is desperate to find an opening so it is very important to protect your eyes and staying in a place of purity. Be aware of what you expose your eyes and ear gates to. I learned that I could not watch certain shows or movies because it opened doors for demonic spirits to infiltrate my eyes. It is important to watch what you listen to because when music is processed in the mind, it turns itself into a mental image. These images can be demonic or soulish and can contaminate your vision, dream and sleep realm.

Be sure to constantly cleanse your eye and ear gates from anything of this world seen and unseen, so you will not have to deal with unnecessary warfare and with trying to decipher whether a dream is demonic, worldly, or soulish.

Jesus will train and show you how to lock and destroy doors, how to chain gates, and how to shutdown demonic portals through visions and dreams. This strategic blueprint will be laid out before you in God's timing.

> *Matthew 116:19 – New King James Version - And I will give you the keys of the kingdom of heaven, and whatever you bind on earth will be bound in heaven, and whatever you loose on earth will be loosed in heaven.*

When you pray into your visions, attempt to describe what you are seeing as much as possible. For example:

> *I see an angel dancing in the spirit. I know it is an angel of peace that I am to release to dance over the assignment in my personal prayer time.*

Sometimes we may not know the English term of what we see and that is okay. Ask for the spirit of wisdom and the spirit of knowledge to come forth and minister to you so you will know what you are seeing, and what you are to pray for to release the vision into the earth realm. If you allow the Holy Spirit to take over your mouth you will decree forth words you have never used or may not have heard of before. You will notice that when you write your visions down and pray into them, they will begin to manifest into the natural, because you have established them into the foundations of the earth.

> *Job 22:28 – New King James Version - You will also declare a thing, and it will be established for you; so light will shine on your ways.*

Sharing Visions

God will reveal to you what visions you are to share with the body of Christ and what you are to keep between you and Him. Visions are prophetic words in the form of images and it is a way God speaks to us. God will give you a prophetic vision of someone but will tell you not to tell the person at that time. You'll know in your heart when it is time to release the vision because you will be synchronized with the timing of God. Do not get ahead of God and share when He is not leading you. People may not be able to handle what you see and sharing with them God is not leading can cause offense, jealousy, and confusion. Remember you have God's eyes. God sees all yet He does not tell of what He sees. We are to be like Him and discern when to share the keys and strategies of our visions versus the vision itself. If there is any hesitancy in your spirit, do not share and wait until God gives you peace about what to release.

Godly & Demonic Visitation

It is important to govern our dream and vision realms and to learn how to be interactive in our dreams and visions. This will enable to us:

- To commune with God in our dreams and visions
- To know when God is wanting us to get up and war and intercede
- To know when dreams and visions are not of God, are demonic in nature and that the enemy is infiltrating our dreams to attack us
- To know when we are having a divine visitation from God versus having a dream or vision
- To know when we are experiencing a demonic visitation from devils, ghosts, astral projectors, sex demons, terrors (fear demons), destiny killers (demons sent to kill or cause us to self-destruct) versus having a dream or vision

In *1Kings 3:5-13*, we find Solomon responding and making his desires known to God in a dream.

> *In Gibeon the Lord appeared to Solomon in a dream by night: and God said, Ask what I shall give thee. And Solomon said, Thou hast shewed unto thy servant David my father great mercy, according as he walked before thee in truth, and in righteousness, and in uprightness of heart with thee; and thou hast kept for him this great kindness, that thou hast given him a son to sit on his throne, as it is this day. And now, O Lord my God, thou hast made thy servant king instead of David my father: and I am but a little child: I know not how to go out or come in.*
>
> *And thy servant is in the midst of thy people which thou hast chosen, a great people, that cannot be numbered nor*

*counted for multitude. Give therefore thy servant an
understanding heart to judge thy people, that I may
discern between good and bad: for who is able to judge
this thy so great a people? And the speech pleased the
Lord, that Solomon had asked this thing. And God said
unto him, Because thou hast asked this thing, and hast
not asked for thyself long life; neither hast asked riches for
thyself, nor hast asked the life of thine enemies; but hast
asked for thyself understanding to discern judgment;*

*Behold, I have done according to thy words: lo, I have
given thee a wise and an understanding heart; so that
there was none like thee before thee, neither after thee
shall any arise like unto thee. And I have also given thee
that which thou hast not asked, both riches, and honour:
so that there shall not be any among the kings like unto
thee all thy days.*

In constantly meditating upon God and perfecting His
image within our imagination, we can discern and respond
to God's voice even when we are sleeping and dreaming,
and we are able to commune with Him. God gives me a
lot of strategies for ministry assignments, ways to combat
the enemy, and even answers and prophetic words in my
sleep and dreams. I am able to get up and write them
down and return to communing with God and even back
to sleep. This is because I have cultivated this part of my
life with God. I expect God to talk to me even in my sleep.
Sometimes, I ask Him to speak to me in dreams and
visions or just to commune with me as I sleep. Because I
am expecting to hear from God, my Spirit is activated to
respond and I do not see it as an inconvenience when I
have to get up and journal, prayer, or fellowship further
with God.
It is important to note that God will also use us in dreams
and visions to war and combat the enemy. God will also
take us in the heavenlies at night to war and intercede.

Ephesians 6:12 - For we wrestle not against flesh and blood, but against principalities, against powers, against the rulers of the darkness of this world, against spiritual wickedness in high places.

<u>High</u> is *"epouranios"* in the Greek and means:
1. above the sky, celestial, heavenly, high
2. existing in the heaven, things that take place in the heaven
3. the heavenly regions
   a. heaven itself, the abode of God and angels
   b. the lower heavens, of the stars,
   c. the heavens, of the clouds
4. the heavenly temple or sanctuary
5. of heavenly origin or nature

Sometimes God will require us to armor up and literally enter the heavenlies to contend with these high places. God will lead us in war and intercession through dream and vision realms or by SHIFTING us into the heavenlies to combat these forces.

If you are like me, you may have had experiences of being in the heavenlies and in high places but not know the reason or purpose. This has caused great warfare, confuse, demonic attacks and even caused fear of going to sleep, praying, and not wanting to be used of God. This is an area in the body of Christ where teaching is needed so we will know that God does use us in this nature, and that He can teach us how to operate in the heavenlies to take down these high places for His glory.

If you are like me, today I cleanse and break you of your frustration, false or misperceived mental illness, hurt from people and warfare, and SHIFT you into knowing that this is part of your calling and God wants to use you powerfully to beat devils and wickedness down. I declare the revelation in this chapter will SHIFT you into the victor and successful kingdom ambassador of every realm that is attached to your destiny.

Even as God will use us to contend with the enemy, the enemy will also attack us in dreams and visions and through demonic visitations. It important to learn when it is God releasing information about the demonic realm through visions and dreams, and when it is the enemy attacking. It is also important to learn how to counterattack, and even to be proactive in our dreams to avoid attacks.

I have a lot of dreams and visions that reveal secrets, revelations, and strategies about the enemy's camp and how to infiltrate those strongholds. These are not sweet precious dreams. They are usually filled with witches, covens, high places, demons, evil people, and border on being nightmares. I would attest that I could write my own horror movies and put Hollywood to shame.

Many in the body of Christ are having these same dreams and visions, but are ruling them as nightmares and/or of no relevance because we have been taught that God would not allow us to have such dreams. I used to think that too until I kept having them. At times, I would not just have dreams but be in the spirit realm, visiting these locations, combating demons and witches and on and on. When I would share my experiences, many would contend I was possessed or mentally ill. As I have considered this over the years, I believe many are misdiagnosed as mentally ill. They have similar experiences as I have, but because there is no or minimal teaching and a fear of exploring such revelation, we medicate and bind up people to try to stop these experiences rather than search God regarding them.

> *Proverbs 3:24-26 - When thou liest down, thou shalt not be afraid: yea, thou shalt lie down, and thy sleep shall be*

sweet. Be not afraid of sudden fear, neither of the desolation of the wicked, when it cometh. For the Lord shall be thy confidence, and shall keep thy foot from being taken.

The word *fear* in this scripture is *"pahad"* in the Hebrew and means, *"sudden alarm, terror, dread, great dread, an object or thing of dread."*

> ### The Amplified Version
> *When you lie down, you shall not be afraid; yes, you shall lie down, and your sleep shall be sweet. Be not afraid of sudden terror and panic, nor of the stormy blast or the storm and ruin of the wicked when it comes [for you will be guiltless], for the Lord shall be your confidence, firm and strong, and shall keep your foot from being caught [in a trap or some hidden danger].*

In this passage of scripture God promises that if we are not afraid when we lie down, our sleep will be sweet. He encourages us to not be afraid (startled, alarmed, caught off guard) of sudden terror and panic. And that He will even keep our foot firm and from being overtaken.

- **These terrors can be a demon, sudden fear due to challenging situations, or just a panic of fear that hits us out of nowhere.**
- **These sudden terrors can come during the day and at night while we are sleeping.**
- **The Hebrew word for *foot* is *"regel"* and means *"to be able to endure, haunt, journey, keep pace."* These terrors come to haunt us, steal our journey; prevent us from keeping pace in God. They will try to kill and overtake us and hinder, thwart, and scar us from walking in the calling that is on our lives or even just functioning daily in life.**

- **These terrors will make us feel as though we have done something wrong, but God tells us *"you will be guiltless."***

If you are not participating in any unrepentant sin, witchcraft and idolatry that may cause these attacks to occur, knowing you are guiltless is important when experiencing these attacks. I say this because the enemy and people will make you feel like you have done something wrong or opened a door, and that is the reason they are occurring. I have been accused of all kinds of things in my effort to acquire deliverance from demonic dreams, visions, and demonic night attacks and visitations. These accusations only caused me to be more fearful, more frustrated, and angry with people who should have been able to help me, and with God who I expected to deliver and protect me. I had to realize that these attacks and encounters where due to and a part of the calling on my life. When I received and accepted that revelation, I begin to cleanse myself of the anger, condemnation, and shame and guilt that I carried. Then with the help of the Holy Spirit, I begin to teach myself how to reign over my night and dream realms and be proactive in my attacks against the enemy.

Psalms 91:1-6
He that dwelleth in the secret place of the most High shall abide under the shadow of the Almighty. I will say of the Lord, He is my refuge and my fortress: my God; in him will I trust. Surely he shall deliver thee from the snare of the fowler, and from the noisome pestilence. He shall cover thee with his feathers, and under his wings shalt thou trust: his truth shall be thy shield and buckler. Thou shalt not be afraid for the terror by night; nor for the arrow that flieth by day; Nor for the pestilence that walketh in darkness; nor for the destruction that wasteth at noonday.

In *Psalms 91*, David is declaring that he dwells in the secret place (covering) and shadow (presence) of God. This secret place and shadow possess:

- God's protective wings (feathers)
- God's covering (refuge)
- God's force field or hedge (fortress)
- God's revelation (shield)
- God's truth (buckler)

David is also declaring that because of God's covering and presence, he will be delivered from and will not fear:

- The snare of the fowler (traps)
- The noisome pestilence (aggravating and pesky demons and experiences)
- The pestilence that walks in darkness (sicknesses, afflictions, demons, ghosts, astral projectors which are people witches, warlocks who translate themselves in the spirit realm to do harm or for thrills, evil lurking in the dark or behind the scenes of life)
- The terror by night (fear, dread, demons and situations that haunt us)
- Arrows that fly during the day (situations, word curses, witchcraft, demonic attacks that hit out of nowhere and for no apparent reason)
- The destruction that waste at noon day (situations and demons that come to cause you to destruct)

Since David is in the secret place, what reason does he have to remind himself or make a declaration that God will surely deliver him and that he should have no fear? That's a great question. I was challenged by the realization of what David was experiencing despite being in the secret place (covering) and shadow (presence) of God.

One of the things I learned from life and *Psalms 91* is that snares, pestilences, terror, arrows, and efforts of destruction are inevitable. Because of the increase of wickedness in the world, we can expect them to continually be a part of the world. We do not like to be afraid, attacked or to feel that we lack control what happens to us. Though we live in this world and can be affected by the challenges of this world, we are not of this world (**Ephesians 2:6-7**...*we are seated in heavenly places with Christ Jesus*). We therefore, must change our mindsets and approach to the experiences of this world, so we can avoid being overtaken by fear and dread of them occurring.

> **John 16:33** - *These things I have spoken unto you, that in me ye might have peace. In the world ye shall have tribulation: but be of good cheer; I have overcome the world.*

> **New Living Translation** - *These things I have spoken to you, so that in Me you may have peace. In the world you have tribulation, but take courage; I have overcome the world.*

We have to SHIFT from a position of worrying and dreading, to knowing that terror and tribulation resides in the world, yet God is all around us and has us. The more we "*take courage*" and yield less to fear and dread, the more we will experience God's peace, covering, protection, deliverance, refuge, fortress. We do this by consistently practicing a lifestyle of courage, while trusting and receiving God's shield (revelation) and buckler (truth). God has overcome the world and has control over every situation in our lives.

Psalms 91:9-12 - Because thou hast made the Lord, which is my refuge, even the most High, thy habitation. There shall no evil befall thee, neither shall any plague come nigh thy dwelling. For he shall give his angels charge over thee, to keep thee in all thy ways. They shall bear thee up in their hands, lest thou dash thy foot against a stone.

Dictionary.com defines *"befall"* as:
1. to happen or occur
2. to come as by right
3. to happen to, especially by chance or fate.

From this definition, we can contend that because God is our refuge and habitation, nothing is happening to us without God knowing it or without His permission. We see further in the scripture that God even has angels directly assign to further guard and uphold us.
As we sleep at night, the enemy will attack us with nightmarish dreams and demonic visitations but he is already defeated. He is also a coward for waiting until we are sleep to pounce on us. That alone let us know that the enemy is afraid of us and knows he only can agitated and instill fear in us. He has no power to overtake us as if he did, he would not have to hit us when we are sleep or when we least expect it.

1Peter 5:8-10 - Keep a cool head. Stay alert. The Devil is poised to pounce, and would like nothing better than to catch you napping. Keep your guard up. You're not the only ones plunged into these hard times. It's the same with Christians all over the world. So keep a firm grip on the faith.

Devils are defeated! God has me and is for me! I reign in God and every devil is cowering in agony under my feet.

Kingdom Awareness Regarding Dreams,
Visions and Demonic Attacks

This chapter will discuss demons and considerations to be aware of regarding dreams, visions and demonic attacks.

- *Shapeshifters* – are demons that can change their form to appear as any person living, dead, or fictional. Initially, shapeshifters appear harmless (cats turning into lions and attacking) or even look like someone you know. It will then turn into a demon or evil thing in the dream and attack you. Shapeshifters are very subtly in dreams and tend to attack when they get you to a place of trusting them or thinking you are safe and have no reason to be alarmed. Be discerning as shapeshifters will attempt to draw you to places in a dream where you will be harmed, attacked, or all of a sudden you are being chased and running for your life.

- *Familiar Spirits* that work in dreams and visions look like someone you know, but really are demons. Though familiar spirits will look and sound familiar, they will not have the character or personality of the person you know, will not act the way the person would normally act. They will be trying to get you to do things that are contrary to God or to what is for you, and will not be for you in the dream.

- *Witch (female sorceress) - Warlock (male sorcerer)* - Witches and warlocks tend to release their spells and attacks in the night. They use translation and astral projection to enter the heavenlies to work their spells and bind people. You may encounter a witch or warlock when God leads you to go into the heavenlies to intercede and pray. Witches and warlocks will immediately attack you when they see you. They are territorial, and will attempt to assert authority over their sphere of influence. They will see the light of God in you and assume you are there to judge them or overtake their sphere. They will attack in effort to protect themselves. Some witches and warlocks will repent and even give their life to God. Some will be sold out to the devil and will stand their ground and fight. Ask God to lead you in how to deal with witches and warlocks.

- God may have you cast them out of the heavenlies
- God may have you physically fight them
- God may tell you to have them repent and give their life to Him as He may want to use them for the kingdom
- God may tell you to have them decide whether they choose to repent or die as in the bible God has little tolerance for witches and warlocks – *"Exodus 2:18 18 Thou shalt not suffer a witch to live."* Some witches and warlocks are sold out for Satan and will choose death because they will refuse to repent. Be sensitive to what God is leading you to do and do not be afraid - for greater is God's power in you than in them.

- *Astral Projectors* - witches, warlocks, or regular people who separate their soul from their physical bodies so they can travel around the heavenly realms. Though demons can attack you sexually at night, sometimes these attacks are astral projectors. They are real people translating themselves into the spirit realm to rape and molest people. They do this for thrills or just because, or to feed an altar or satanic power. Sometimes, when people have encounters in their home where they see shadows, figures of people, or things moving around, these are not always what we call ghosts or demonic entities. Astral Projectors love to scare and play tricks on people. They are thrill seekers at the expense of the general public who like to act as if these types of experiences only occur in movies. As you become keener in discernment, and being interactive in your dreams, you will be able to discern whether you are dealing with demons or astral projectors. Most astral projectors will flee if you threaten to cut their silver cord. The cord is what connects their soul to their body and they can literally die if they are disconnected from it. They also flee from rebukes in Jesus name and the blood of Jesus. If they do not respond to a rebuke or threat of cutting their cord, they are most likely a ghost or a territorial spirit that has some connection to that region or place. This would require a cleansing of the land and building to rid of these attacks.

> *Ecclesiastes 12:5-7 Also when they shall be afraid of that which is high, and fears shall be in the way, and the almond tree shall flourish, and the grasshopper shall be a burden, and desire shall fail: because man goeth to his long home, and the mourners go about the streets: Or ever the silver cord be loosed, or the golden bowl be broken, or the pitcher be broken at the fountain, or the wheel broken at the cistern. Then shall the dust return to the earth as it was: and the spirit shall return unto God who gave it.*

- *Spiritual Weapons* - Sometimes you may require spiritual weapons to combat in your dreams and visions or when God use you in the heavenlies.

2Corinthians:10-4 – For the weapons of our warfare are not carnal, but mighty through God to the pulling down of strong holds.
New International Version - *The weapons we fight with are not the weapons of the world. On the contrary, they have divine power to demolish strongholds.*

Weapon in the Greek is *"hoplon"* and means:
1. Utensil or tool (offensive for war)
2. Armor, an instrument
3. Any tool or implement for preparing a thing arms used in warfare
4. Arms used in warfare, weapons

Warfare in the Greek is *"strateia"* and means:
1. Military service, i. e. (figuratively) the apostolic career (as one of hardship and danger): — warfare.
2. An expedition, campaign, military service, warfare
3. Paul likens his contest with the difficulties that oppose him in the discharge of his apostolic duties, as warfare

- Moses had a rod
- Ezekiel had the power of clapping hands
- Joshua had treading feet
- David had worship and the power to decree and declare – He had five smooth stones
- In the bible God has used or has threatened to use hail, fire, torrent winds, swords, scalpels, threshing instruments and on and on

- Jesus had to word and was the word and carried the government of God upon His shoulders
- We all have literal swords and the sword of the word

All through the bible we see how songs, sounds, dance and movement, praise, shouts, claps, rods, decreeing, scepters, etc., are used in warfare. God uses the foolish things to confound the wise (*1Corinthians 1:27, Psalms 8:2*). Though God can use fleshly instruments, His weapons embody His spiritual nature and character. This means that the weapons God gives us, manifests from the spirit realm and from the reality and truth of who He is. Not from the world, our flesh, or our truth or perception. God's weapons manifest from His truth and His Spirit. (My book entitled, "*Atmosphere Changers*" yields revelation on weapons used in warfare and intercession).

Ask God to assign weapons to you and do not be afraid to call for weapons in your dreams and visions, when in the heavenlies, and during times of warfare and intercession. This is important as the devil will be threatening you with knives, guns, swords, and weapons you never seen before. But God's weapons are greater and He has even bigger and more advanced knives, guns, swords, etc. God can do great things with the simplest of weapons, so do not limit or box Him.

> ***Jeremiah 51:20*** *- Thou art my battle axe and weapons of war: for with thee will I break in pieces the nations, and with thee will I destroy kingdoms.*
>
> **English Standard Version**

*You are my hammer and weapon of war: with you
I break nations in pieces; with you I destroy
kingdoms.*

The Message Version - *God says, You, Babylon,
are my hammer, my weapon of war. I'll use you to
smash godless nations, use you to knock kingdoms
to bits.*

God's weapons are for the purposes of smashing,
judging, destroying, demolishing, extinguishing,
and dismantling strongholds, while conquering
over the enemy.

God will use us and the very fashion of movement
and expression of our existence as war club - a
battle axe, to bring about His purpose and justice.

Battle axe in the Hebrew is *"mapes"* and means *"a
smiter, war club, club, a hammer."*

Isaiah 41:15-16 - *Behold, I will make thee a new
sharp threshing instrument having teeth: thou
shalt thresh the mountains, and beat them small,
and shalt make the hills as chaff. Thou shalt fan
them, and the wind shall carry them away, and
the whirlwind shall scatter them: and thou shalt
rejoice in the Lord, and shalt glory in the Holy
One of Israel.*

Prophetically and even naturally, mountains are high
places or positions and thoughts of pride and idol
worship. God is saying I will transform you into a
threshing sledge that has teeth and you will trample and
tear down mountains (the high places that exalt against
me). And then you will use your hand to fan (disperse,
winnow) the mountains. Your fanning hand -winding

arms, shall be like a wind, even a whirlwind - a hurricane that scatters the mountains for my glory.

Whewwwwww!

Even as God use us as weapons, He has a **storehouse of artillery**.

> *Jeremiah 50:25 NLT* - *The LORD has opened his armory and brought out weapons to vent his fury. The terror that falls upon the Babylonians will be the work of the Sovereign LORD of Heaven's Armies.*
> **The Amplified Version** - *The Lord has opened His armory and has brought forth [the nations who unknowingly are] the weapons of His indignation and wrath, for the Lord God of hosts has work to do in the land of the Chaldeans.*
>
> *NET Bible* - *I have opened up the place where my weapons are stored. I have brought out the weapons for carrying out my wrath. For I, the Lord GOD who rules over all, have work to carry out in the land of Babylonia.*
>
> **The Message Version Verse 25-26**
> *I, God, opened my arsenal. I brought out my weapons of wrath.*
> *The Master, God –of–the–Angel–Armies, has a job to do in Babylon.*
> *Come at her from all sides! Break into her granaries!*
> *Shovel her into piles and burn her up. Leave nothing!*
> *Leave no one!*

I believe this storehouse - arsenal of artillery, resides in us through the Holy Spirit as well as in heaven. **ASK GOD FOR WEAPONS! The devil cannot handle God's arsenal.**

- Sometimes when you wake up from dreams or demonic attacks, you may feel fearful, panicky, tired, drained, filthy, sick, confused, disoriented, bound, depressed, lonely, worried, lustful, sexually aroused, etc. None of these attributes are of God. Use the blood of Jesus and the fire of God to cleanse yourself as these negative attributes have been deposited in your soul, mind, emotion, and body while you dreamed or slept, and can affect your day to day life. You will be trying to figure out why you feel scared or panicky; it maybe because you spent the night being chased in your dream. Cleanse these things from your soul, mind, emotions and body so they will not have any control over you when you are awake.

Being Proactive & Asserting Authority
Over Dreams, Visions and Attacks

- Practice a lifestyle respecting that fear is a part of life but that you do not have to be fearful. Practice a lifestyle being courageous, keeping cool, firm in the faith, and not dreading the experience of demonic dreams and visions and demonic attacks. The enemy feeds on our fear and frustration. These negative attributes can become a door opener to breeding more unnecessary attacks.
  - Consistently declare out scriptures and pray prayers that build up your identity and authority regarding who you are in God
  - Be careful what you watch and listen to and be open to giving up whatever is necessary that will open doors to unnecessary attacks and demonic dreams
  - Be proactive in maintaining and cultivating the presence of God and an open heaven over your life and home
  - When traveling, take time pray over the room you will sleep in. Some of your attacks could be because you are susceptible to demons in the territory, things that happened before you entered place or region, or because of other peoples' issues.

- Accept that Godly dreams, visions and Holy Spirit encounters are a part of your walk as a believer.

- Command your Spirit to be sensitive to God and to hearing His voice and experiencing His presence as you sleep.

- Expect to have encounters with God. As you lay down to sleep every night, soak yourself in the blood of Jesus and power of God, and as you meditate upon Him, ask Him for prophetic dreams and visions and divine downloads as you sleep. Be okay with getting up to pray, journal, and further commune as God leads you. Trust that if God gets you up, He will sustain you where you can still function and be refreshed during the day.

- Though we do not accept demonic dreams and attacks, it is important to accept everything that may come with our calling. Jesus had to accept that He was going to be persecuted and die on the cross for our sins. Paul had to accept a thorn in his side. I had to accept that God was allowing these experiences so I would one day share this information with you and be prepared and prepare others for end time warfare. (**Romans 8:18** - *For I reckon that the sufferings of this present time are not worthy to be compared with the glory which shall be revealed in us*). Ask God to give you understanding regarding the reason this is a part of your calling and to teach you how to assert authority in this area of your life.

- As you are meditating on God, command your brain and Spirit to remember and retain all dreams and visions.

- Pray against the spirit of the dream stealer who comes and zaps your dreams, preventing you from remembering them.

- Declare to your body, soul and mind that you will not fear demonic activity, but will remain in a place of peace and courage, while asserting all authority over the enemy when asleep or awake.

- Command your Spirit to be so sensitive to the atmosphere around you and that you will immediately wake up and be in a place of confident authority when a demon, witch, warlock, or astral projector is present.

- Also declare that even if you are attacked while sleep, you will not respond in fear. Declare that you will SHIFT to a posture of peace and confidence, while commanding whatever is attacking you to loose you and to be immediately cast out of your sphere of influence in Jesus name.

- After being attacked in your sleep, cleanse yourself of all fear and anything else the enemy attempts to impart into you. Many sexual attacks come to instill lust, perverse thoughts and desires, shame and guilt. Cleanse out these impurities and command your righteousness to be restored in Jesus name.

- As God leads you, counterattack any devil, witch, warlock, astral projector that attacked you in your sleep. I will add some scriptures at the end of the chapter that you can use as God leads to BAM the devil. Send angels to judge and war against devils that attack you. Using the blood of Jesus and the fortress (force field) of God, close any doors, portals, gateways, to which demons maybe entering. If necessary, repent for any sin that caused open doors and judge every illegal attack by letting devils, witches, etc., know they are illegal and you torment them for their actions in Jesus name.
- Command your Spirit to be active and interactive in your dreams and visions. Declare that as you dream, you will be fully aware of what is occurring and will be so keen in your dreams that you will discern all familiar spirits and shapeshifters.

- If you find yourself running or being chased in your dreams, command your spirit to take authority in the dream and to stop running. Remember fear is not your portion. Because dreams occur in real realms, you have the power to assert authority over dreams and change them. Depending on what is going on in a dream, I will call for angelic assistance, chase whatever was chasing me, and beat down whatever attacking me. I may also command myself to wake up, especially if I feel I am unsafe in a dream. I then cleanse myself of all fear, anxiety, and any traumatic events or tragedy the enemy is trying to instill in my life, and then I will ask God to send angels to deal with what occurred in the dream, while praying against whatever was attacking me in my dream.

- Some dreams manifest in real life because we do not counterattack them in prayer. Immediately cancel all demonic words and assignments in dreams involving accidents, tragedies, death attempts, loss of jobs, houses, income, health issues, etc

Sweet Sleep Declaration

Psalms 91

I dwell in the secret place of the most High and abide under the shadow of the Almighty. I say of LORD, You are my refuge and my fortress: my God; in You I trust. Surely you have deliver me from the snare of the fowler, and from the noisome pestilence. You have covered me with You feathers, and under Your wings I do trust: Your truth is my shield and buckler. I am not afraid of the terror by night; nor for the arrow that flieth by day; Nor for the pestilence that walketh in darkness; nor for the destruction that wasteth at noonday. A thousand has fallen at my side, and ten thousand at my right hand; but it will not come nigh me. Only with my eyes do I behold and see the reward of the wicked.

Because I have made You LORD, which is my refuge, even the most High, my habitation; there shall no evil befall me, neither shall any plague come nigh my dwelling. For You Lord have given your angels charge over me, to keep me in all my ways. They bear me up in their hands, lest I dash my foot against a stone.

I tread upon the lion and adder: the young lion and the dragon I trample under feet. Because I hath set my love upon You God, You have delivered me: You have set me on high, because I know Your name. When I call upon You, You answer me: You have and will deliver me out of trouble; You have honored me and shown me the protection and covering of your salvation.

1. As a *Kingdom Heir,* I decree that I have power over all the power of the enemy whether awake, sleep, in my dreams, and within the spirit realm (Luke 10:19).
2. For I undoubtedly know that weapons of my warfare are not carnal, but mighty through God to the pulling down of strongholds. Even in my sleep, I cast down imaginations, and every high thing that exalts itself against the knowledge of God, and bring into captivity

every thought, intent, devise, and action to the obedience of Christ (2Corinthians 10:4).

3. I decree I am well balanced, temperate, sober of mind, vigilant and cautious at all times, even when asleep; such that my enemy cannot seize upon me to devour my destiny (1Peter 5:8).

4. I stand on Isaiah 54:17 and declare that no weapon that is formed against me shall prosper, in season or out of season, when I am sleep or in a place of rest; and contend that the Lord eternally condemns every tongue, instrument, and demonic entity that rise against me. This is my heritage because I am a servant of You, Lord.

5. I assert my God given authority as a *Kingdom Heir*, and decree a keen sensitivity to detect dangers seen and unseen. I decree that just as in everyday life, I have power to perpetually arrest, disrupt, and halt ungodly dreams and demonic attacks; even to the point of taking immediate authority within my dreams and the spirit realm, while changing and shifting them to a place of deliverance, healing, and victory.

6. When I lie down, I am not afraid; yes, I shall lie down, and my sleep will be sweet. Whether asleep or awake, I am not afraid neither of sudden terror and panic, nor of stormy blasts or the storm and ruin of the wicked.   For You Lord are my confidence, firm and strong, and You are keeping my destiny from being caught in demonic and soulish traps or hidden dangers of the enemy (Proverbs 3:23-26).

7. I repent for sins personally and generationally; sins committed in my household, upon my land, and sphere of influence. I close all doors spiritually and naturally to nightmares, generational idolatry, familiar spirits, night terrors, the boogieman, ghosts, invaders, feeders, perversion, rape, and molestation spirits, night visitors, witches, warlocks, astral projectors and demonic

attackers, spirits of death and hell, demonic harassment and stranglers (Matthew 5:25).

8. I receive forgiveness and decree a freeing from all anxiousness, worry, fear, stress, anger, hatred, unforgiveness, uncleanness, trauma, etc., and decree a cleansing and freeing from any soulish and emotional areas that would give way to the enemy.

9. For I do not fret or have any anxiety about anything, but in every circumstance and in everything, by prayer and petition (definite requests), with thanksgiving, I continue to make my wants known to my God. And my God's peace has become a tranquil state within my soul. I am assured of my salvation through Christ. And so, fearing nothing and being content with my Kingly inheritance, I decree that His peace, which transcends all understanding is garrisoning and mounting a powerful guard over my heart and mind and is brooding wholeness and wellness in me. (Philippians 4:6-7).

10. I therefore cancel all dedications, covenants, rituals, hexes, vexes, enchantments, bewitchments made to demons and idols, witches, warlocks, wicked people, as it relates to me personally, generationally, my land and sphere of influence, and the spiritual gifts in my family lineage (Numbers 4:18).

11. I close every, door, gateway and portal, spiritually and naturally, to demonic dreams, astral projection and my spirit man being subjected to ungodly summons in the night. I fully resist the devil and decree I only harken to the unction and voice of my King Jesus (James 4:7).

12. I plead the blood of Jesus over me, my home, my bed, my covers, my atmosphere, my possessions and sphere of influence and decree that to the pure, in heart and conscience, all things are pure (Titus 1:15).

13. As born again *Kingdom Heir*, I decree I am covered by the purified blood of Jesus and solidified in the all-powerful name of Jesus - the name that is above every

name - the name to which every knee shall bow and every tongue should confess that My Jesus is Lord and savior unto the glory of God my Father, Refuge, Shelter, and Protector (Philippians 2:8-11).

14. Even now I cleanse my body, mind, spirit, soul, thoughts, emotions, personality, character, will, and sphere of influence of all tragedy, infirmity, affliction, fear, worry, weariness, tiredness, frustration, failure, depression, loneliness, double mindedness, unbelief, perversion, demonic seeds, pollution, imprints, impressions (*speak forth whatever negative attributes have been planted through dreams and demonic night attacks*). I decree a complete cleansing and healing through the blood of Jesus and the matchless name of Jesus and command every seed, root, manifestation, harvest, stench and stain of these ungodly attributes to be annulled. You are destroyed, rendered powerless and zapped to nothing by the declarative name of Jesus (Proverbs 23:7).

15. For there is no torment in love. God grants sleep to those He loves. I am consumed by God's perfect love which causes Him to sustain and comfort me as I sleep (1 John 4:18, Psalms 42:8, Psalms 127:2)

16. Angels are protecting and working on my behalf as I rest and sleep (Psalms 34:7, 91:11).

17. I decree that instead of demonic activity and hellish dreams, God instructs me in the night season (Psalm 16:7).

18. For it is God's desire for me to know the mysteries of the kingdom of heaven. I therefore declare that as I sleep, I shall not only awaken refreshed, but shall have prophetic dreams and visions and receive kingdom keys, strategies, and heavenly downloads from my God. These revelations shall expose the enemy, release answers, direction, cures, and understanding, change life, build faith, shift atmospheres, overtake regions,

and produce and establish the glory of God in the earth (Matthew 13:11).

19. Even in my sleep, I take up the yoke of the Lord. Your yoke is comforting, delivering, healing, revitalizing, strengthening, empowering, elevating, activating and releasing fulfillment to my royal lineage and destiny (Matthew 11:28).

20. I shall arise proclaiming that my sleep was sweet, for I have been fruitfully blessed and nourished in sweet heavenly sleep (Jeremiah 31:26).

PEACE! Not As The World Gives

1. I the name of Jesus, decree that I receive my heavenly reality of unshakable peace from You, Jesus. Peace! Not as the world gives. But peace that comes from the very DNA of my heavenly home (John 14:27).
2. As a *Kingdom Heir*, I thank You for imparting Your peace into me, for leaving it with me, and for encouraging me to embrace the power, authority, aroma, nature and heavenly reality of peace.
3. I reject the trials and tribulations of this world. Even when challenging situations occur, I remain in a tranquil state of peace.
4. I continually seek You for my purposed destiny and I am open to walking out naturally what has already occurred in the spirit realm. I say burdens, oppression, and mental anguish are not my lot. And even when being persecuted for righteousness sake, I remained grounded in the purpose of my destiny. I remained consecrated in the vigor of peace.
5. For You, Christ Jesus have continuously reminded me and demonstrated through the fulfillment of Your work at the cross, that the world has been conquered.   As a *Kingdom Heir, I,* too, have subdued, prevailed, overcome and conquered this world.
6. I am victorious and assert my victory! I decree I am more than conquerors through Christ Jesus who loves us. *I am uncompromisingly persuaded beyond a doubt (am sure) that neither death nor life, nor angels nor principalities, nor things impending and threatening nor things to come, nor powers, nor height nor depth, nor anything else in all creation will be able to separate me from the love of God which is in Christ Jesus my Lord* (Romans 8:38-39).
7. Though the enemy devises his strategies, they are thwarted. He proposes his plans, yet they will not stand. I rebuke the strategies of the enemy while

declaring exemption from rage of demonic havoc and war. I spew out peace!

8. God thwarts the plans of the crafty so that their hands achieve no success, for God is with me. He has given me complete, sound, surpassing peace. Such peace yields a state of security and order in my sphere of influence...harmonizing all that concerns me (Job 5:12, Isa 8:10).

9. Plan and plot all you want--nothing will prosper. All your talk is mere babble, empty words with no fruit; because when all is said and done, the last word is Immanuel--God-With-Us. He is my voice, my reality, my temperament, my peace.

10. Call your councils of war, but they will be worthless. Develop your strategies, but they will not succeed. For God is with me! I still myself in the call to trust the Lord, I still the storms of life with my validity of peace (Isa 8:10).

11. In Jesus name, I call forth a mutual concord of agreement between my heavenly government and the government of this world. I declare silence upon the hostilities that attempts to steal, destroy, dismantle and displace the calm felicity of my assertive peace.

12. For You Lord, have ordained, orchestrated, delegated, and declared the judgment and laws of my surroundings. I am established in Your peace (Isaiah 26:12).

13. You guard me and keep me in perfect and constant peace because my mind - both its inclination and its character – stays centered in You; I am committed to You, lean on You and hope confidently in You (Isaiah 26: 3).

14. Your peace is a fruitful weapon that proclaims my spiritual supremacy. It isn't conditional, flawed, empty or temporary, like the world gives. It is a silent vengeance evaporating the wretched storm. I declare Your supernatural gift of peace.

BAM The Devil Scriptures

Psalms 109:29 - *Let mine adversaries be clothed with shame, and let them cover themselves with their own confusion, as with a mantle.*

> **New Living Translation** - *May my accusers be clothed with disgrace and wrapped in shame as in a cloak.*

> **The Message Version** – *Let them be jeered by the crowd when they stand up, followed by cheers for me, your servant. Dress my accusers in clothes dirty with shame, discarded and humiliating old ragbag clothes.*

Psalm 35:26 - *May all who gloat over my distress be put to shame and confusion; may all who exalt themselves over me be clothed with shame and disgrace.*

Psalm 109:18 - *He wore cursing as his garment; it entered into his body like water, into his bones like oil.*

Psalms 109:17-20 - *Yes, he loved cursing, and it came [back] upon him; he delighted not in blessing, and it was far from him. He clothed himself also with cursing as with his garment, and it seeped into his inward [life] like water, and like oil into his bones. Let it be to him as the raiment with which he covers himself and as the girdle with which he is girded continually. Let this be the reward of my adversaries from the Lord, and of those who speak evil against my life.*

As he loved cursing, so let it come unto him: as he delighted not in blessing, so let it be far from him. As he clothed himself with cursing like as with his garment, so let it come into his bowels like water, and like oil into his bones. Let it be unto him as the garment which covereth him, and for a girdle (belt, strength) wherewith he is girded continually. Let this be the reward of mine adversaries from the Lord, and of them that speak evil against my soul

Psalms 40:13-15 - Be pleased, O Lord, to deliver (defend, rescue) me: O Lord, make haste to help me. Let them be ashamed and confounded (embarrassed, reproached) together that seek after my soul to destroy it; let them be driven backward and put to shame that wish me evil. Let them be desolate for a reward of their shame (confusion) that say unto me, Aha, aha.

> Desolate is "samem" in the Hebrew and means "to be desolate, be appalled, stun, stupefy, horrored, horror-causer, deflowered, ravaged, astounded, ruined."

Psalms 35:4-12 – Let them be confounded (delayed, disconcerted) and put to shame that seek after my soul: let them be turned back and brought to confusion that devise my hurt. Let them be as chaff (driven out, rubbish, waste) before the wind: and let the angel of the Lord chase them. Let their way be dark (miserable) and slippery (treacherous): and let the angel of the Lord persecute them. For without cause have they hid for me their net in a pit (destruction, corruption, a grave), which without cause they have digged for my soul.

Let destruction come upon him at unawares; and let his net (is reset in the Hebrew and means trap or judgment) that he hath hid catch himself: into that very destruction let him fall. And my soul shall be joyful in the Lord: it shall rejoice in his salvation. All my bones shall say, Lord, who is like unto thee, which deliverest the poor from him that is too strong for him, yea, the poor and the needy from him that spoileth him? False witnesses did rise up; they laid to my charge things that I knew not. They rewarded me evil for good to the spoiling of my soul.

Psalm 63:9 - Those who want to kill me will be destroyed; they will go down to the depths of the earth.

Psalm 71:13 - May my accusers perish in shame; may those who want to harm me be covered with scorn and disgrace.

Psalm 119:95 - *The wicked are waiting to destroy me, but I will ponder your statutes.*
Psalms 60:12 - *Through God we will do valiantly, for it is He who shall tread down our enemies.*

Psalms 125:3 - *For the scepter of wickedness shall not rest on the land allotted to the righteous, lest the righteous reach out their hands to iniquity."*

Psalms 27:5-6 - *For in the time of trouble He shall hide me in His pavilion; in the secret place of His tabernacle He shall hide me; He shall set me high upon a rock. And now my head shall be lifted up above my enemies all around me; therefore I will offer sacrifices of joy in His tabernacle; I will sing, yes, I will sing praises to the Lord.*

Jeremiah 14:3 - *The nobles send their servants for water; they go to the cisterns but find no water. They return with their jars unfilled; dismayed and despairing, they cover their heads.*

Job 8:20 - *They that hate thee shall be clothed with shame; and the dwelling place of the wicked shall come to nought.*

Deuteronomy 28:7 - *The Lord will cause your enemies who rise against you to be defeated before your face; they shall come out against you one way and flee before you seven ways.*

Isaiah 54:17 - *No weapon formed against you shall prosper, and every tongue which rises against you in judgment you shall condemn. This is the heritage of the servants of the Lord, and their righteousness is from Me," Says the Lord.*

Isaiah 41:11-12 - *Behold, all those who were incensed against you shall be ashamed and disgraced; they shall be as nothing, And those who strive with you shall perish. You shall seek them and not find them - Those who contended with you. Those who war against you shall be as nothing, as a nonexistent thing.*

1John 4:4 - *You, dear children, are from God and have overcome them, because the one who is in you is greater than the one who is in the world.*

Luke 10:19 - *I have given you authority to trample on snakes and scorpions and to overcome all the power of the enemy; nothing will harm you.*

Romans 16:20 - *The God of peace will soon crush Satan under your feet. The grace of our Lord Jesus be with you.*

Romans 8:37-39 - *No, in all these things we are more than conquerors through him who loved us. For I am convinced that neither death nor life, neither angels nor demons . . . will be able to separate us from the love of God that is in Christ Jesus our Lord.*

James 4:7 - *Submit yourselves, then, to God. Resist the devil, and he will flee from you.*

1John 3:8 . . . *The reason the Son of God appeared was to destroy the devil's work.*

Mark 6:7 . . . *Calling the Twelve to him, he sent them out two by two and gave them authority over evil spirits.*

Luke 10:17 - *The seventy-two returned with joy and said, "Lord, even the demons submit to us in your name."*

Matthew 16:19 - *I will give you the keys of the kingdom of heaven; whatever you bind on earth will be bound in heaven, and whatever you loose on earth will be loosed in heaven.*

Matthew 28:18 - *Then Jesus came to them and said, "All authority in heaven and on earth has been given to me. Therefore go. . . ."*

John 14:12 - *I tell you the truth, anyone who has faith in me will do what I have been doing. He will do even greater things than these, because I am going to the Father.*

Malachi 4:3 - *And you shall tread down the wicked; for they shall be ashes under the soles of your feet in the day that I shall do this, saith the Lord of hosts.*

References

Scripture references are from:
www.biblegateway.com
www.blueletterbible.com
www.crosswalk.com
www.Wikipedia.com

Definitions are quoted from:
www.answers.com
www.m-w.com
www.dictionary.com

**Book Cover was designed by Reenita Keys.
Connect with her via Facebook.**

Kingdom Shifters Books & Apparel

Available at <u>Kingdomshifters.com</u>

BOOKS FOR EVERYONE

Healing The Wounded Leader

Kingdom Shifters Decree That Thang

There Is An App For That

Kingdom Watchman Builder On the Wall

Embodiment Of A Kingdom Watchman
Releasing The Vision

Dismantling Homosexuality Handbook
Feasting In His Presence

Kingdom Heirs Decree That Thing

Let There Be Sight

Atmosphere Changers (Weaponry)

BOOKS FOR DANCERS

Dancers! Dancers! Decree That Thang

Spirits That Attack Dance Ministers & Ministries

TEE SHIRTS

Kingdom Shifters Tee Shirt

Let The Fruit Speak Tee Shirt

Releasing The Vision Tee Shirt

Kingdom Perspective Tee Shirt

Stand in Position Tee Shirt

No Defense Tee Shirt

My God Rules Like A Boss Tee Shirt

Destiny Blueprint Tee Shirt

CD'S

Decree That Thing CD

Kingdom Heirs Decree That Thing CD

Teachings & Worship CD's

Printed in Great Britain
by Amazon